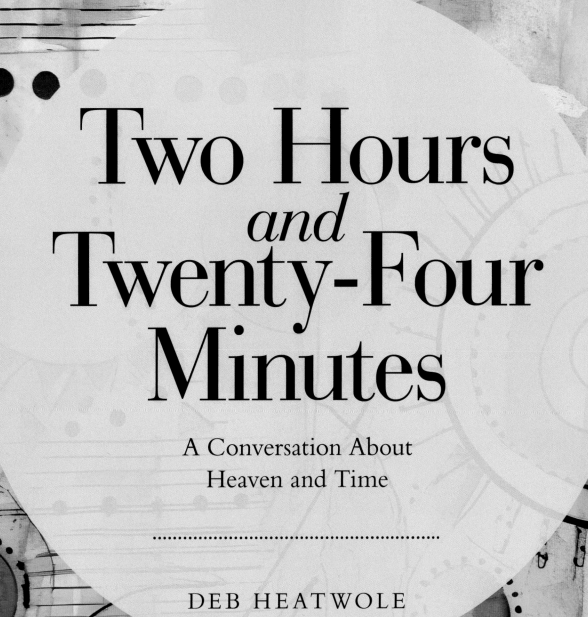

Two Hours *and* Twenty-Four Minutes

A Conversation About Heaven and Time

DEB HEATWOLE

WestBow Press books may be ordered through booksellers or by contacting:

WestBow Press
A Division of Thomas Nelson & Zondervan
1663 Liberty Drive
Bloomington, IN 47403
www.westbowpress.com
844-714-3454

New International Version (NIV)
Holy Bible, New International Version®, NIV® Copyright ©1973, 1978, 1984, 2011
by Biblica, Inc.® Used by permission. All rights reserved worldwide.

Coordinating pages by Susan Bailey RetroResortdesign
Interior Image Credit: DigiEyeArt
Page 50 original cross by Mike Heatwole

ISBN: 979-8-3850-2774-3 (sc)
ISBN: 979-8-3850-2775-0 (hc)
ISBN: 979-8-3850-2776-7 (e)

Library of Congress Control Number: 2024912482

Print information available on the last page.

WestBow Press rev. date: 01/31/2025

WestBow
PRESS
A DIVISION OF THOMAS NELSON
& ZONDERVAN

This book is dedicated to Lavonne.
When I think of you, I think of
SUNSHINE!
From me to you with so much love…

Now to Him who is able to do immeasurably more than all we ask or imagine, according to His power that is at work within us.

Ephesians 3:20

A Conversation About Heaven and Time

Fear not for I am with you. Isaiah 41:19

The thing about time is…
we never have enough of it.
We never know when we will be called
off of the train, this train we call life.

BELIEVE

Will it be when we turn 33?

That's not enough time!

PEACE

What about when we're 56?

~~~~~~~~~~~

That's not enough time!

Will it happen when we reach 74 or 85?

—————∞∞∞—————

That still isn't enough time!

Hope is the thing with feathers that perches
In the soul and sings the tune without words
And never stops at all. –Emily Dickinson

You see, time is an Earth thing.
It's a kind of measurement.
Time is a way to keep track of
our lives.

"For I know the plans I have for you," declares the lord," Plans to prosper you and not to harm you, Plans to give you hope and a future." -Jeremiah 29:11

Seconds to minutes

Minutes to hours

Hours to days

Days to months

Months to years

Years that make a lifetime.

Be strong and courageous. Do not be afraid; do not be discouraged, for the Lord your God will be with you wherever you go. -Joshua 1:9

Our Earthly time is not like the time God has for us in Heaven. Let's stop for a minute and talk about this place called Heaven.

JOY

Heaven is a special place.
The Bible tells us that Jesus
went there to
prepare a place for us, a place
where we will spend eternity!

⌘

"I go to prepare a place for you."
John 14:2

He made everything beautiful in its time. He has set eternity in the human heart; yet no one can fathom what God has done from beginning to end. -Ecclesiastes 3:11

He made Heaven with his precise and amazing design. In Heaven, the streets are made of gold and the gates of pearls.

※※※※

The twelve gates were twelve pearls, each gate made of a single pearl. The great street of the city was of gold, as pure as transparent glass.
-Revelations 21:21

How precious to me are your thoughts, oh god! How vast is the sum of them. -Psalms 139:17

Think about how beautiful the Earth is. It is hard to imagine just how magnificent Heaven will be. He made Heaven just for us!

WE SING HALLELUJAH!

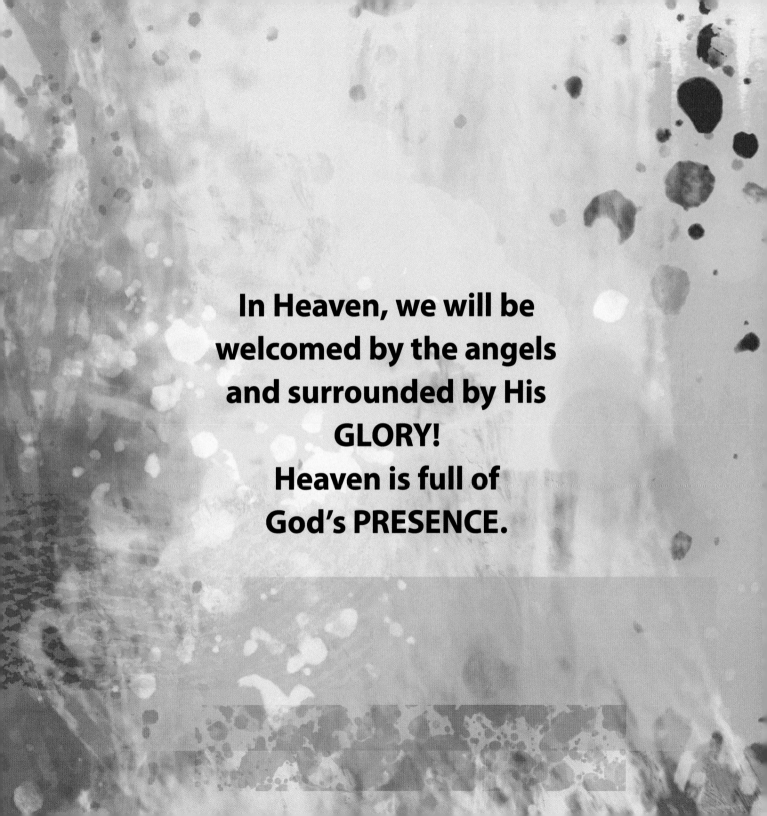

In Heaven, we will be welcomed by the angels and surrounded by His GLORY!
Heaven is full of God's PRESENCE.

He will cover you with his feathers, and under His wings you will find refuge. -PSALMS 91:4

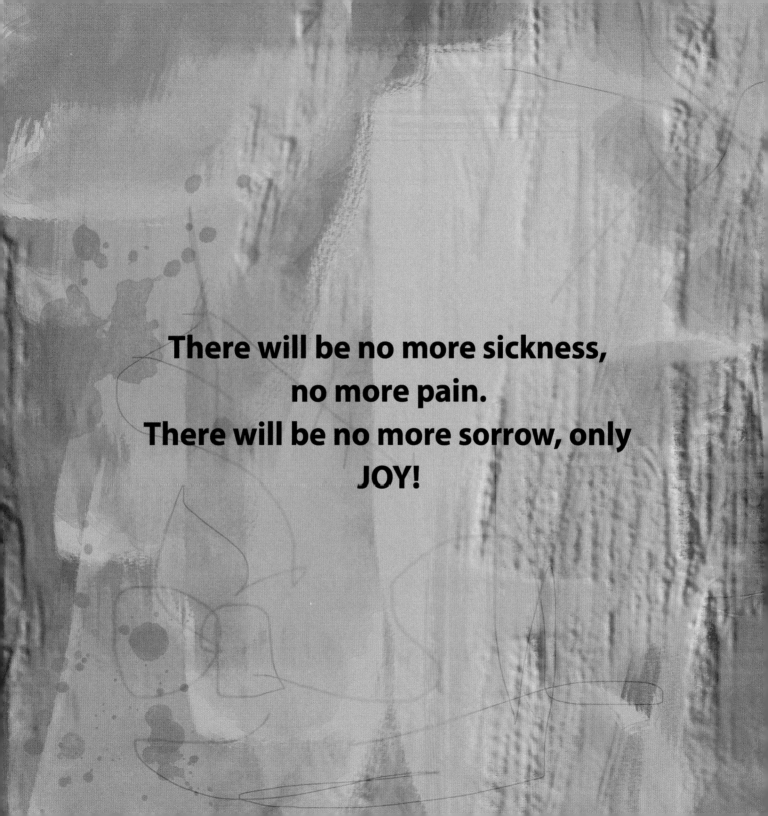

There will be no more sickness,
no more pain.
There will be no more sorrow, only
JOY!

WORSHIP THE LORD WITH GLADNESS. COME BEFORE HIM WITH JOYFUL SONGS. PSALM 100:2

I believe that we will fall to the ground on our knees in WORSHIP!
We will SING, SING, SING at the top of our lungs!

Let them praise his name with dancing. -Psalms 149:3

We will experience LOVE
like we never have before!
We are going to DANCE
with our hands lifted high
when we get to
Heaven!

Faith is the substance of things hoped for the Evidence of things not seen. - hebrews 11:1

Time in Heaven is much different than it is here on the Earth. In Heaven, one thousand years is like a day.

ONE THOUSAND YEARS IN
HEAVEN IS EQUAL TO A SINGLE
DAY ON EARTH!
THIS IS HEAVEN'S TIME!

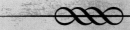

But do not forget this one
thing, dear friends:
With the Lord a day is like a thousand years,
and a thousand years are like a day.
2 Peter 3:8

REJOICE AND BE GLAD

Have you ever gone for just
a day without your family?
That is the time God promises
it will be until we see
them again in Heaven!

In Heaven, a thousand years are like a day. No one lives for a thousand years, but some may live for a hundred. One hundred years will seem like TWO HOURS AND TWENTY-FOUR MINUTES. God made time in Heaven just for us. In the blink of an eye, our loved ones will join us. With arms wide open, we will be there to welcome them to their new home ...Heaven.

Time

We learn that love is time and time is love. We leave behind the love we gave away to those closest to us on this journey. We will live in their hearts and in their lives as they pass this part of us on to their loved ones.

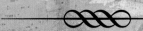

God, thank you for the time you gave me with my loved ones.

Forgiveness

As we collect our years, we learn that by forgiving others, we are really freeing ourselves. We find that it is much harder to forgive ourselves than it is to forgive others.
Let it GO.

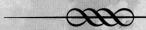

God, I come to you to ask for your forgiveness, not just for me, but for all of those I need to forgive.

Peace

Life teaches us that real peace lives inside us and has nothing to do with our circumstances. We know that the peace that God puts in our hearts is everlasting. He says, "Be still, and know that I am God".

God, please quiet my heart and fill me with your peace.

"Be still, and know that I am God."
Psalms 46:10
(Notice the comma after be still!)

FOR GOD SO LOVED THE WORLD THAT HE SENT HIS ONLY SON, THAT WHOSOEVER BELIEVES IN HIM SHALL NOT PERISH BUT HAVE EVERLASTING LIFE. —JOHN 3:16

Prayer of Salvation

Dear Heavenly Father, thank you for sending your Son, Jesus, into the world. You sent Him so that we could be forgiven and spend eternity in Heaven.
Forgive me of my sin and fill my heart with your presence.
Fill me with your love and your peace.
Fill me from the inside out. Thank you for the promise of eternal life.
Thank you for Heaven.

A Psalm of David

The Lord is my shepherd, I shall not be in want. He makes me lie down in green pastures, He leads me beside quiet waters, He restores my soul. He guides me in paths of righteousness for His name's sake. Even though I walk through the valley of the shadow of death, I will fear no evil, for You are with me; Your rod and Your staff, they comfort me. You prepare a table before me in the presence of my enemies. You anoint my head with oil, my cup overflows. Surely goodness and love will follow me all the days of my life, and I will dwell in the house of the Lord forever.

Psalm 23

Psalm 121

I lift up my eyes to the mountains-
where does my help come from?
My help comes from the Lord,
the maker of Heaven and Earth.
He will not let your foot slip-
He who watches over you will not slumber;
indeed, He who watches over Israel
will neither slumber nor sleep.
The Lord watches over you-
the Lord is your shade at your right hand;
the sun will not harm you by day,
nor the moon by night.
The Lord will keep you from all harm-
He will watch over your life;
the Lord will watch over your coming
and going both now and forevermore.

The Lord's Prayer

Our Father which art in Heaven,
hallowed be Your name,
Your kingdom come,
Your will be done,
on earth as it is in Heaven.
Give us today our daily bread.
And forgive us our debts,
as we also have forgiven our debtors.
Lead us not into temptation,
but deliver us from the evil one.
For Yours is the kingdom and the
power and the glory forever.
Amen!
Matthew 6: 9-13

Epilogue

God's plan for us included Heaven and Earth, but that wasn't all. He saw our hearts. He knew how much we miss the people we love, so he created time.

Earth's time and Heaven's time are so different. He purposed it that way just for us. The Bible tells us that 1000 years in Heaven is equal to 24 hours on the Earth. We won't live a 1000 years, but we might make it to 100, which is a tenth of a 1000. A tenth of 24 hours is 2.4 hours. 2.4 hours is two hours and twenty-four minutes.

100 Earth years will seem like 2 hours and 24 minutes when we get to Heaven. God sped up the time in Heaven so that when we go there, we won't have any time to miss our loved ones. They will be there with us before we know it. That is God's promise to us.

He made Earth's time so much slower to give us more time with our loved ones here. He knew we could never have enough of it. 100 years here is 36,500 days. We live day by day by day. We have TIME, a gift from the God who loves us more than we could ever imagine.

We have the assurance that when this life comes to an end here on the Earth, we will only have to wait two hours and twenty-four minutes for our loved ones to join us. Together we will spend eternity in Heaven.

Father in Heaven, thank you for the gift of time on Earth and in Heaven. Thank you for loving us so much. You have given us time to spend with our loved ones here on Earth. Here, time is much slower. Thank you for speeding up time in Heaven so that our loved ones will join us before we have time to even miss them. You made time in Heaven so fast that we won't have to wait. Before we know it, we will be there to welcome them with arms wide open.

Printed in the United States
by Baker & Taylor Publisher Services